Homeowners Guide To

Handling an Insurance Claim

Making Sense of the Insanity

A complete guide to handling your insurance claim and getting paid what you are supposed to.

Help? I have an insurance claim... now what do I do?

Copyright @2010. Revised 2020

All rights reserved. No material in this book may be reproduced or utilizing any form or by any means, electronic or mechanical, including photocopying, recording or by any information storage or retrieval system, without permission from the author.

Forward

Hello, my name is "Nobody", I will let you know right now that this is NOT my real name. Why not use my real name? Because I am a real currently working Catastrophe Insurance Adjuster, also known as a CAT Adjuster. I could, but then I would never work as an Insurance Adjuster again. I am a working Independent Insurance Adjuster. I am licensed in over 13 states at any given time.

You see what I am about to tell you has NEVER been put in one place before for the average person to read. The world of insurance, on its surface, seems really complicated but it's not so long as you have the right information. If you take time to read this book AND get your policy out with it, by the time you are done you WILL know more about your insurance policy, the claims process and how to manage your claim than not only the average person but also most claims adjuster...without question!

I am going to break down EVERYTHING for you so that YOU, the one that pays the Premium for your insurance, are equipped to not only understand your policy and your claim, but you will absolutely get paid what you are supposed to get paid for and not one penny more or less.

I have worked in the insurance industry for over 35 years now. I started out working with my father in an Insurance Restoration Construction company, owned my Restoration Construction company with 40 employees and have been an Independent Insurance Adjuster for over 19 years and now at this time of the revisions of this book my wife and I own an insurance agency. As a contractor I have dealt with everything from small water damages, auto's that impacted buildings, major water damages because of broken pipes, fire damage, floods, old, windstorms, hail, freeze claims, tornado damage to multi-story commercial fires and hurricanes. As an Independent adjuster I have done and seen it all. I have spent years traveling to different parts of the country working every natural disaster you can imagine.

I am going to open the lid on EVERYTHING insurance for you so that you are equipped to deal with the Insurance Company, The adjusters supervisor, the adjuster, the contractor in order to understand and get exactly what you are supposed to get and not a penny more. I am going to speak plainly and honestly so that you completely understand everything about dealing with your insurance company.

Read this book first, all of it before you file a claim, mark it up and let it be your guide in to coming to a successful conclusion of your insurance claim.

BEFORE YOU FILE A CLAIM MAKE SURE YOU HAVE A COPY OF YOUR POLICY, READ IT, KNOW WHAT IS COVERED AND THEN FILE THE CLAIM. I will be referencing parts to your policy, so it is important to have a copy handy. If you do not have a copy call your agent and get a copy. Most insurance carriers today give you the ability to access the policy online, so check their website.

Here's What To Do When You Think You Have A Claim.

1. Stop, breath and relax.
2. Do not rush out and file the claim immediately.
3. Know what your policy and rights are before you go in. If you have a question, ask your agent first and get clarification. If you need a copy of your policy, then request it from the agent. MAKE you agent work for you, do not let them send you off to somewhere else to get answers.
4. If you do not know what your deductible (see the section on deductible below) call your agent and ask, know this before you file the claim.
5. Start taking pictures of everything now, especially what caused the damage, like a broken pipe or the hole in the ceiling.
6. Go to the end of this book and fill out the "Claim worksheet" first!

Understand that the insurance company will want to make sure that the damage you have is a "COVERED PERIL" before they commit or extend coverage. What this means they will not pay you a dime until they know you are covered.

If there was a theft a police report will be needed, and this can take from a few days to a couple of weeks depending on the police department. If it was a fire, then a report from the fire department will be needed. However, none of these reports will be needed to determine coverage and get money, this is the job of the adjuster to determine. They are the ones to interpret coverage and then submit for payment. Do not let them lag on this. If you need emergency money, then request it.

What Is Insurance...A Basic Overview To Understanding

Definition of Insurance is:
"A promise of compensation for specific potential future losses in exchange for a periodic payment. Insurance is designed to protect the financial well-being of an individual, company or other entity in the case of unexpected loss."

The Policy

I am going to be talking specifically about your homeowner's policy.

NOTE: *You're understanding and knowing your policy is the greatest power you have. Why would anyone rely on the interpretation of a legal document by the person or the company that will ultimately have to give you money?*

Property Insurance is basically a form of gambling where you pay money to a company in exchange for a position against "a named peril" like a wind event or whatever the peril is, happening and causing damaging what you own. In order to be protected against this "Peril" the peril must be listed in your policy under "covered perils". If the peril is not listed it is not covered….maybe.

Go get your Insurance policy right now. Keep in mind each insurance company is a little different on their headings and what they call things. Once you have it thumb through it and look only at the bolded headings. Get familiar with these headings. I want you to do is find the section on "what's covered".

Go to the "perils or what's covered" section, get familiar with it. Look at what you are covered against. Simple, right? No, it's not. Because you now need to read the section on your policy of what's "NOT" covered.

What's not covered, are events and/or conditions that if they occurs you will have NO coverage and trust me, when that happens you will not be a happy camper because you thought you were covered, if it's not in the policy you are not covered.

An event that people always get upset about for not having coverage is "FLOOD coverage". So, check your policy. If you have questions call your agent to get specifics and update your policy.

If after reading through your policy and seeing what is covered and what's not covered, you have a question concerning coverage that's not covered typically you must get what they call "a rider". A rider is additional insurance that you I don that is specific to an event or item that you want to make sure is covered. But understand to that there's an additional cost for this rider.

Before I move on, I want to mention the one piece of coverage you must have on your policy is "replacement cost coverage". Check your policy now and if you do not have this coverage, run, do not walk, to your phone and call your agent or the company you bought your policy from and add "Replacement Cost Coverage" to your policy. If you do not have this coverage and do not add this coverage you are stupid! Sorry to be blunt but I have seen more people get upset because they did not have this coverage, nor did they understand this coverage. Add **"replacement cost coverage"** to your policy now!

Deductible:
What Is It And How Does It Work?

If you do not know what your deductible is call your agent right now and ask! Your deductible is your contribution to the claim before it's paid by the insurance company. It is designed as a threshold to prevent filing small claims. As a homeowner there are cost of owning a home. My rule of thumb is if your claim is not at least 3 times the amount of the repair cost, then consider not filing a claim, but this only applies to you is your deductible is $500 or less. If your deductible is more than this then you make the decision on whether to file, the claim or not. The reason is, if the claim is not the result of a regional event then filing a claim could go against you at renewal time in determining how much the insurance company is going to increase your premium at renewal or if they are going to cancel you all together. So be aware.

Your deductible will come off the top of the cost of repairs before you receive any money from the insurance company. So, if your deductible is $500 and the repairs are $650 then you will get $150 from the insurance company. Or the cost of repair is $450 you will get nothing. Therefore, IT IS IMPORTANT to get a basic cost of repairs prior to filing a claim. I see this all the time. If you decide to file a claim and then discover the cost is increasing due to unforeseen damage you can always file at this time. For the most part you have two years to file a claim from the date of damage. This is also why you take photos before, during and after repairs to document everything. If you want do video but document everything !!

The "Declarations (DEC) Page"

You are insured up to a specific Policy limits or amounts. These limits are broken down into Coverage's known as Coverage A, B, C and so on. Each coverage type has a limit and these limits can be found on the declarations page of your policy.

Coverage A is your "Dwelling" or your home.

Pay special attention to this. Under coverage A there are provisions of coverage of what is covered and of what is not covered. For example, water damage may be excluded from the "BASIC Policy". If you want, and you do, trust me on this, coverage for water damage you can add a rider to add this coverage. Make sure you ask the agent what riders can be added to the basic policy. For the most part the additional cost the rider is incremental and low.

Additional Living Expenses coverage (ALE)

This coverage is to pay for that in the event you must move out of your home and live somewhere else the cost will be covered. If it's short term then you are probably looking at a hotel, if it's longer it may be needed to move into a rental house or apartment. This is important so read this and take it to heart!! If your home is a 4-bedroom home with 3 baths, then the insurance company MUST pay for the same level or quality of the home you live in. Which means do not let them put you in a Motel 6, with one room, two queen beds, with no kitchen for 6 people and expect you to live there for six months. If you need cloths cleaned, then that to must be paid for. Same goes for your food and eating out. If you food cost is normally $500 a month and you are spending $1,200 a month by being out of your home then the insurance company will cover the overage of the normal cost you spend, so they will pay you $700 for food. Keep all receipts and document everything.

If you need a place immediately then go to a hotel and turn in the receipt to the adjuster. MOST times ALE will be handled by the "Desk Adjuster" assigned to your claim. So get in touch with them and start the process. If you need an advance this is the person to start with. But understand, you may have to go out of pocket for the first few days on the hotel, food and so on until the claim is validated and gets under way.

This is an area where the insurance company will pay as little as possible if they can get away with it.

Coverage B is "Other Structures" on your property such as a barn, shed or a detached garage, any additional structured not attached to the dwelling.

NOTE: Usually there is a maximum limit of coverage these "other structures" regardless of what they cost to replace. This number is "usually" around $10,000. If you have a building on your property that will cost MORE than this limit you need to add a "Ryder" which will increase the limits on THIS building. This rider may or may not be available to add, it depends on the carrier. If it's important to you, find a different carrier to insure with.

Coverage C is your "Contents"

Contents are anything that "IS NOT" connected permanently to the structure. This includes your furniture, close, toiletries, kitchen utensils, dishes and so on. Basically, anything that you've gone to the store and purchased to go into the home.

An example of this would be window coverings such as drapes, they are contents where there are blinds are not. A refrigerator is considered contents, unless it built in, but a dishwasher is not considered contents because it's attached to the structure.

There are special coverage's or limits of coverage's on specific items, such as jewelry, guns, collectables, heirlooms and so on. These types of items on a regular policy may only be insured anywhere from $250 to $2500, that's it!

Depending on your policy these items may or may not be covered only if you declare them or if listed. If you need more insurance on that item, you need to request a "Special Rider" which will increase the coverage to what you want.... but it will cost more.

Your coverage amount on your contents should be as much as the coverage amount on your dwelling. If you have high end furniture, then it could be even more.

Riders

Riders are additional things added to your basic policy or the policy you purchased. For example, Flood coverage. When you purchase you policy ASK the agent what additional coverages are available to add to the policy you are buying. By asking this questions you will now know exactly what coverages are NOT included in your policy. To add coverages usually cost very little, so ask so you can make an informed decision to add this coverage or not.

The worst thing you can do is find out your not covered for something at the time you need it.

Insurance Companies, the Way They Work

Insurance companies are a business and their business is to get people to buy their policies, more polices = more premiums! Once the insurance company sells you coverage then the insurance company moves into the mode of managing "risk". And I won't bore you with the details, but they do this in a variety of different ways.

Insurance companies are much like Las Vegas or Atlantic City casinos. And what I mean by that is, they are not in the business of losing more money than what they bring in.

They deal with the masses but within those masses if they have an entity or an individual that they are paying out more money to then premiums they are paying to the insurance company, that entity or individual is a bad risk and thus their policy will be canceled in very short order.

What You Mean To The Insurance Company

"I have been with my insurance company for the last 30 years (or longer) and have never had a claim so surly they are going to cover me."

If I had a nickel for every time, I heard this statement or one close to it, I would have a lot of nickels.

First off, I hate to disappoint you, but your insurance company does not care how long you have been with them! They do not care if you have ever filed a claim, they only care that you pay the premium on the policy, period! So, if you are not shopping for insurance at least once every couple of

years then you are spending more money than need on less coverage than you deserve. It's that simple!
SHOP, SHOP and SHOP some more.

The Agent

The Agent that sold you your policy should become "a friend". Their phone number should be programmed into your phone because the first thing that you should do, without delay or question is to contact your "Agent". Your agent, if they are a good agent, will want to know what's going on with you. They will want to know if you have dealings with the insurance company. They will also want to know whether you have a good experience your not. Why? Because if you don't have a good experience the chances are you will find another insurance company for your insurance needs and that means the agent loses a client.

The other reason you should contact your agent is because they may have resources to help you deal with your claim a lot easier. The agent will likely have referral sources that you may need to take care of issues. So ask if they can recommended a contractor, roofer, water mitigation company and so on.

You buy insurance for "peace of mind" and your agent is a part of that piece of mind that you purchased. So utilize them.

In order to file a valid claim, the event that caused the loss must be "sudden and accidental" and/or be named peril.

Examples of named peril or which are typically covered for in your policy.

- Wind damage
- Fire damage
- Smoke damage
- Water damage – including freeze coverage
- Theft and vandalism
- Major events such as hurricanes, tornadoes, hailstorms

Depending on your policy there may be differences, but these are some basic coverages of perils.

Filing A Claim For Your Loss

So after you call your agent, and you have taken pictures, pictures, pictures and then take some more pictures, if your agent did not file the claim for you they will give you an 800 number to the insurance company to file a claim. The person on the other end is going to ask you some questions and then assign you a claim number. Once you have that claim number, they are going to assign an adjuster to your claim. That adjuster will contact you and make an appointment with you to come out and investigate the claim. They're going to be looking for a few things. One of which is the "cause of loss" or "COL" for short. The adjuster is going to document the claim by taking photographs, measurements of the room, the roof to whatever is damaged, they will ask for receipts, they may even asked for a recorded statement from you.

Once the adjuster has this information, they will put it in the form of a report and send it up to their supervisor. The supervisor is the one who will make the decision on whether it's a covered loss or not. Once it is determined that it's a valid claim and a covered loss the insurance company will issue payment. This is the claims process in a simplistic way. There are a whole lot of other steps in this process which you will soon discover.

The Adjuster

There are two types of adjusters. The first is a "Staff Adjuster". The staff adjuster is employed by the insurance company and are typically paid a salary. The second type of adjuster is an "Independent Adjuster" and they are not employed by the insurance company. The independent adjuster is typically their own business entity, a subcontractor, to an independent adjusting firm. Insurance companies' contract with independent adjusting firms to handle a variety of different types of claims. Insurance companies cannot keep full-time employees in every market. There simply is not enough business to justify hiring a full-time staff adjuster. This is why insurance companies' contract with independent adjusting firms.

That independent adjuster may adjust claims for several different insurance companies in the area. Independent adjusters are paid based on the size of the claim and/or a fee schedule that has been negotiated between the independent adjusting firm and the insurance company.

Another reason insurance companies contract with independent adjusting firms is for natural disasters or events such as hurricanes, tornadoes, hailstorms, floods and so on. The reason for this is that in most states the insurance company has a limited amount of days to contact their insured once they file a claim. So, the insurance companies will use independent adjusters to start the claims process so that they will be within the law. During a large storm event even with the additional help of independent adjusters they may not be able to make contact within the specified time frames.

Understand that the adjuster that is working on your claim has no powers to make any decisions on whether your claim is covered or not. That adjuster simply documents the claim based on your policy.

Contact with the Adjuster

When the adjuster contacts you secure a contact number, note who their supervisor is and their contact information. If you need to communicate with the adjuster ALWAYS do it via email. You can call or speak with them on the phone, but it is always a good idea to send an email to document your correspondence. If your claim is due to a "large loss event" like a hurricane it may take the adjuster a few days to contact, you and set inspection. During a large loss event the adjuster will have over 50 claims dumped on him in a matter of minutes to start the process. Each person's claim must be contacted one at a time to determine the extent of damage, location of covered property and any immediate needs you may have. The first call may not produce an inspection date but is simply the call first call to log in that you have been contacted.

If for any reason you have a problem with the adjuster go to the supervisor, BUT ONLY IF THERE IS A PROBLEM THE ASSIGNED ADJUSTER IS NOT HANDELING. If you place several calls to the adjuster and they are not getting back with you, call the supervisor.

Depreciation, what the heck is "Depreciation"?

When you file a claim, you are filing a claim to get paid back on what you have lost or what has been damaged. The insurance company is going to take what they call depreciation from the amount of money that the object has been appraised at. That depreciation is based primarily on age although sometimes a percentage basis is used, but let's stick with age.

The older the object is the greater the amount of depreciation. Now this is where that "replacement cost coverage" that I spoke of earlier comes in to play. For example, if you had damage to your roof and the type of roof that is on your house is a 25 year composition shingle. And let's say that the roof material has been on your house since you purchased it 30 years ago, so the 25-year composition shingle is over 30 years old. The insurance company is going to depreciate your roof based on the age. You may ask yourself how do they come up with how old the roof is? They're going to determine this by asking you questions. Questions such as "when did you buy the house?", "Have you ever put a roof on the house?". If you have a roof that has a 25 year life expectancy and its 30 years old, if you do not have replacement cost coverage, you will be paid absolutely zero for that roof because of depreciation, the roof is past his life expectancy.

If you have replacement cost coverage, then you will be paid for that roof regardless of the age. So long as the damage to the roof was caused by a covered peril.

Depending on the laws in your state the insurance company will still take depreciation but it's in the form of "recoverable depreciation" meaning they will hold the depreciation back from you until you have made the repairs. Once you have the roof replaced, you contact the insurance company and they will release the depreciation that was held back to you.

Everything that I've covered thus far are basic information about your insurance policy, the insurance company, the role of the adjuster and the process overall. I want you to understand very clearly everything that you've read up and to this point.

Now on to the reality of managing your claim. And trust me more times than not it's not going to be pretty or very easy.

The "COST" Of Repairing YOUR Home

Have you ever heard the term "framing the argument"? Well that's what I'm going to show you how to do. If you don't get anything else out of this book, you need to get this!

You have had damage to your home and you file a claim the the adjuster, is going to prepare a repair estimate based on a computer program called Xactimate, or another program like it. In this computer program they are going to have what is called "regional pricing". These prices are set or gathered by Xactimate or the other program. The pricing in this program is really skewed towards the insurance companies benefit. Insurance restoration and repair is a very specialized form of construction and the cost of the construction is very different from say a remodel or a new addition to your home. And I say this from having a father that has been an insurance restoration contractor for over 50 years and I have been in the Insurance Restoration Contractor industry for over 25 years either working with my father having owning my own insurance restoration construction company as well as being an independent insurance adjuster for going on 20 years now.

The insurance adjuster will use this program to justify their pricing for the repairs of the damage to your home and it's what you will be paid. Most people when they get this estimate from the insurance company basically take it as gospel in that that is all the insurance company is going to pay. Understand that "nothing is final regarding your claim". And this includes the money the insurance company is paying you for the repairs.

Here's what typically happens after the adjuster inspects your home for damage.

- The adjuster takes his information and compiles an estimate of repairs.
- The adjuster completes his report and forwards it with the estimate, and photos to supervisor.
- The supervisor looks at it and will either approve it or send it back to the adjuster for revisions.

Most of the time those revisions are to lower the amount of money it takes to make the repairs. The supervisor's job is to manage the claim or the loss. They will do this in a variety of different ways.

- Once the file is approved it is sent up for payment which means you will be receiving a check.
- You receive your check, and hopefully a copy of the estimate, and then you freak out because there's not enough money to make the repairs.
- You call the adjuster to find out why the number is so low.

This is basically how it goes. But remember what I said earlier, nothing is final. So, you may be asking yourself "what can I do?". Well, the first thing you need to do, if you want your home repaired correctly, is to hire a contractor. But do not hire a contractor who does not specialize in insurance restoration and repair. If you do you are making a big mistake! Why? An insurance restoration contractor, let me clarify this, a "good" insurance restoration contractor will take the estimate that you received from the insurance company and go over it with a fine tooth comb and they will find things that either the adjuster left out or the supervisor requested the adjuster modify, as well as pricing out the project.

*NOTE: You do not have to or need to get more than one estimate from any contractor. It is completely up to you which contractor that you use to make the repairs to your home.

Why you "SHOULD" use an "Insurance Restoration Contractor"?

Because it is a specialty business and they will be able to handle it correctly and will be able to talk directly to the insurance company concerning your claim. For all intents and purposes, they will represent you. In addition, as they are working on your home if they find additional issues either the insurance adjuster missed, didn't see or uncovered as work proceeded they will be able to present an addendum to the estimate to the insurance company for payment. If you have a contractor that is not experienced in this type of work it will not get repaired correctly or you may have to pay for it out-of-pocket because you simply don't know or understand the process and that the insurance company is still responsible for these cost.

If their code upgrades that must be done to your home as a result of code changes in your area, the cost of these code changes are the responsibility of the insurance company to pay. If you have hired a contractor that does not specialize in insurance restoration that contractor will simply present, you with the bill for you to pay or they may just ignore it altogether and you will never know.

Follow these steps and you will make your life a lot easier.

1. Take photographs and then take more photographs of everything. Inside, outside and of the building. Make sure that the photos are time and date stamped.

2. Locate then contact a reputable Insurance Restoration Contractor in your area.

3. Get the Insurance Restoration Contractor to your home to do an inspection and an estimate. Talk to them, walk through your home with them and let them tell you how the repairs should be made. Once you've done your due diligence and are comfortable, sign with them. These contractors usually have what they called "an authorization form" for you to sign. Sign it! Also make clear to them that any estimate completed will be sent to you first and gone over with you to explain it.

4. Call your agent and let them know you have a claim to file. The agent should file it for you. If not, they agent will give you an 800# to call the carrier yourself. The representative should give you a claim number at that time.

5. An adjuster should call you within 24 hours to set a time to come and inspect.

6. You may want to have the contractor at this meeting so that they can walk through the claim with the adjuster

and explain what must be done to make repairs. The adjuster and your contractor will meet at your home and do a walk-through so that they get what is called an "agreed-upon scope of work". Allow the contractor to handle everything at this point. You may even want the contractor to call and schedule the inspection with the adjuster.

Follow these steps and you will save yourself time and a few headaches.

The Good And The Bad Of Using A Restoration Contractor

Make sure "YOU" find and hire the restoration contractor. Do not allow the insurance company to refer one to you. They will tell you that you can use ANY contractor you want, BUT the adjuster will tell you the contractor refers will do the work for what the adjuster has estimated. Key word is "estimated".

If you can avoid it do not use a contractor on the insurance companies "approved list" or one they refer to you. What this typically means when a contractor is on the insurance companies approved list is that they will do the work the adjuster has laid out and make repairs the way the insurance company wants them to be made. You may end up paying them but make no mistake about it that contractor does not work for you they are working for the next referral from that adjuster or from the insurance. Which brings me to the next point.

Paying the Contractor

A restoration contractor, unlike a neighborhood contractor or remodel contractor, while start repairs prior to the issue of payment and will typically carry the cost of the project until the insurance company issues payment. This is a big help and will ensure that you receive the depreciation for the work being done. If you use a remodel or neighborhood contractor, they are going to want payment upfront before the work is done and when it is completed.

Make sure that you control payment to the contractor. Do a final walkthrough with the contractor before final payment is issued.

Also, make sure the contractor carries insurance and request that you be named an additional insured on their policy. This will entail receiving a certificate with all the information about their policy and who to contact in the event of an event.

What it means to be additionally insured is that if ANYTHING happens on your property concerning the contractor, this means if one of their people get hurt, their insurance will take care of it. If you do not have this certificate if anyone gets hurt on your property they are coming after your insurance.

PROTECT YOUR ASSETS!

One More Thing About Insurance Restoration Contractors

Most Insurance Restoration Contractors want to take care of you and to do the best work possible. Most of them will take care of problems immediately. But you, the homeowner, must communicate with them and understand what repairs are going to be done and what's not going to be done. You, the homeowner can sometimes have unrealistic expectations concerning your home. For example, if a wall in your home is crooked because of the framing it will not be straight because of new drywall. If your roof has bumps in it because of the sheathing, decking and framing it is going to have bumps in it after new shingles are put on it. If there's a scratch on the floor before the work starts and no work is being done on the floor than the scratch is still going to be there. If the insurance company is paying for $100 light fixture and don't expect the contractor to replace it with a $200 light fixture without paying for the increased cost. If you want upgrades and I would encourage you to explore upgrades at this time, just be prepared to pay for them out of your pocket.

Don't be one of those homeowners that wants their 20 or 30 or 50-year-old home to be a new home. Give the contractor a break, communicate with them because issues will arise, employees will screw up and you will get upset during this process. Relax and communicate with your Contractor. And finally, when it comes time to pay the contractor for his work, pay him. Most Insurance Restoration Contractors carry the job financially in its entirety until the insurance company pays. Most all insurance restoration companies that I know of take care of their clients in a very timely manner and will always take care of any problems.

How Does The Insurance Company Come Up With The Cost To Repair Your Home?

The computer program, Xactimate, that I spoke of has been around since 1986. Make no mistake about it this program the insurance companies use is geared towards insurance companies benefit. The database of cost in this program does NOT reflect your contractors pricing. Every contractor is different and their cost of doing business is different. The Insurance Restoration Contractor that is licensed, has insurance and will stand behind their work. They should have a modified price list of what "their" cost are. Xactimate pricing or any other pricing software the insurance companies use is nothing more than a guideline. It is by no means written in stone, although the adjuster may try to tell you that it is.

If the insurance company tells you, they will not pay any more than what is on their estimate then they are breaking all sorts of laws and insurance regulations, one of which is "price-fixing".

So, to recap. If your goal is to have your home repaired correctly and back to pre-loss condition then find an insurance restoration contractor in your area and meet with them. If you like them and are comfortable with them after you've checked them out, sign the authorization and then let them communicate with the insurance company on your behalf.

If your goal is simply to get paid on your claim and NOT to repair your home or get it repaired as cheaply as possible in order to put money in your pocket, then do not contact an insurance restoration contractor. Find a local contractor and tell them what you want.

Mistake number one: Hiring Family or Family Contractor to make repairs to your home.

For the most part I recommend that you DO NOT use a family member or family friend who is a contractor to make repairs to your home. If you want problems and possibly ruin a relationship with the family member you are hiring, other family members, and/or problems with the repair process and/or the quality of repairs then go ahead and hire "Uncle Bob" as your contractor. Any issues they are going through or if they do not show up when they are supposed to or not at all, you are supposed to understand because we are family or friends. If you go against this rule you are asking for problems from the start. **Do not do it!!!**

Remember, reconstruction to your home as a result of fire, water, wind or any other peril is a specialized field and you need a company that is a specialist in the industry of Insurance Restoration.

Getting paid for what is cost to make repairs.

Ok, here's the deal. For the most part, Insurance companies will pay you what they need to to make you happy. If they can get away with paying you a dollar for five dollars in damage and you are happy with the that, or better yet ignorant of that, they will. Hear me on this. IT IS UP TO YOU TO SUBSTANCIATE YOUR CLAIM AND WHAT IT WILL COST (Remember this phrase, write it down) to put you "Back to PRE-LOSS Condition ". If you've done the correct thing and hired a restoration contractor you are ahead of the game.

But for kicks and grins let's just assume that you haven't done the correct thing. Let's say the insurance company is not paying you what you think you are entitled to according to your policy as you interpret it. You have a couple of options.

Option #1: The Attorney

The first option is to hire an attorney and typically there are attorneys that specialize in insurance claims. Most of the time attorneys get involved with insurance claims after a major event such as a hurricane or maybe hailstorm and after the insured has received money from the insurance company.

Attorneys will come in to the area and advertise to people that if they been paid for their insurance claim and feel it's not fair than to call them and they will represent you, typically at no cost to you up front, and deal with the insurance company on the backend to get you more money. Depending on the State you live in will depend whether that money to the attorneys paid by you out of the additional claim money that you get or whether they are paid by the insurance company directly.

If you hire an attorney for your claim, they are typically filing what is called a "bad faith" claim, but only after they have tried to negotiate to get it settled. If the claim is settled, then the attorney will get a percentage of the settlement they negotiate. If a "bad Faith" claim is filed, then the insurance will pay the attorney fees. Remember that attorneys will take a case only if they feel they will get paid.

These are your options legally. Anytime you get involved with an attorney it is a headache and you can expect it to take a while to settle the claim. And when I say a while, I mean it could be two or three years before your claim is settled. Once you hire an attorney your claim is immediately turned over to the insurance companies' legal department so they can talk attorney talk. One of the tools the attorney uses in dealing with your claim is time. The longer the claim is open the more it will cost the insurance company and thus the more agreeable they become in getting it closed.

Option #2: The Public Adjuster Or Better Known As "A Wolf In Sheep's Clothing" And By The Way "Bend Over Please!"

Now here's a subject dear to my heart. Have you ever had a person used the term "trust me"? And you did! How that turned out for you? How does a public adjuster work? When you sign with the public adjuster to handle your claim they are going to take, and I stress the word "take", a minimum of 10% and probably closer to 30 of your money right off the top from dollar one. Their sales pitch is they will charge 15-30% commission or fee and you will get back more than that because they are involved. To this I say, this is absolute and utter bullshit!

First off, they are not going to spend the time or effort on your claim to get you an extra 10 to 30% or more above and beyond your claim amount the insurance company is already going to pay. It's just simply not worth it to them. Once you sign with the Public Adjuster, they have already made their money. Once they take their commission or fee then you are left with less than what is the cost to make your repairs to your home. In addition, as a result of you signing with the public adjuster the insurance company is required to place their name along with yours on the insurance draft. So even if you have a dispute with them you can't do anything with the draft because the public adjuster must sign off on the draft before it can be even cashed.

And in many circumstances, it is in their contract that you must sign the draft or insurance check over to them and they will issue you a check for the balance of what they think you are owed.

This is how Public Adjusters work. First off, once you sign a contract with the public adjusting firm may have already made their money. All communication from your insurance company must go through the PA's firm, they are your legal representative for this claim. Once the PA makes contact with the insurance adjuster an appointment will be scheduled to do a walk through at your home. The PA will have had contacted or have contractors that they work with to provide them with estimates of the repairs on your home to present the insurance company to substantiate the increased cost of your claim. They either pay these contractors a small fee for writing an estimate or they will try to get you to sign with the contractor to do the work with the promise that the contractor will make all the needed repairs for whatever's left after their fees are paid. And if you believe this, I have a bridge I want to sell you.

Understand this, construction cost are construction cost and every contractor must make a profit in order to stay in business. They must maintain a license, insurance, Workmen's Comp and so on. If a public adjuster takes upwards of 30% plus possibly cost, there is no way for a contractor to do the repairs to your home for what is left.

One of two things are going to happen. You are either going to pay additional money to the contractor basically the money the public adjuster took as his percentage or he is going to take shortcuts on materials and labor to fit his business model. If they do the work for money is left any shortcuts that they've taken you won't even know about for weeks, months or even years after they are gone.

Why do I have such strong opinions about public adjusters? Both as a restoration contractor and independent adjuster I have seen more and heard more horror stories concerning public adjusters than you can shake a stick at. The short of it, public adjusters screw people more than they help people. Are there times when a public adjuster is needed? Yes, but very rarely and only on claims that are complex, and you simply don't want to deal with it.

If you hire a public adjuster understand what you are hiring. You are hiring a public adjuster because of convenience and you simply do not want to deal with the claim yourself.

Hiring a public adjuster is much like hiring an attorney. Do not hire these individuals thinking that you are going to end up with more money in the end. More times than not they are going to cost you money.

Most low-level public adjusting firms are simply out there to make an easy buck off of your claim. They get as they say "the low hanging fruit".

If you are absolutely hellbent on hiring a public adjuster this is how you should approach them.

1. Deal with the insurance company yourself, allow the adjuster to come out and inspect your home and complete his estimate of repairs.
2. Then wait to receive your draft or check from the insurance company.
3. If you feel you are still owed more money, argue with the insurance company as far as you can. Send in estimates

and documents to justify this. Maybe they send you more money maybe not, but remember "you" have to substantiate why you are entitled to more money for your claim.

4. Once you feel you have exhausted every avenue with the insurance company then call the public adjuster and tell them you want to hire them. When they come out to meet with you there going to ask you to sign a contract. On that contract is going to state they are entitled a percentage from "dollar one" on the claim. Even the money you have already received!

5. Tell them to modify that to reflect they will receive their percentage ONLY on the amount of money they are able to get above and beyond what the insurance company has already paid on the claim.

NOTE: 99% of the public adjusters will not take your claim based on what I've just laid out. Why? Because of low hanging fruit has already been gathered by you and it will simply not be profitable for them to spend time on the claim that may get you an additional $100 or even $10,000. You are much better served and having a qualified and skilled Insurance Restoration Contractor work on your behalf with the insurance company because they are dealing with facts and actualities on your claim.

However; if by chance they take your claim under these circumstances then you have nothing to lose and everything to gain.

Option #3

There is a massive need to help people with their claims, to make sure that they are getting what they are entitled to. If you want something that is simple and straight forward as well as have the information in hand in order to deal with your insurance adjuster, we provide the following service.

You can hire us as your claim consultant, and it will not cost you an arm and leg. We work very simply like this.

Once you file your claim or if you're in the middle of your claim contact us for a free consultation. We will spend about 30 minutes with you and look at the validity of your claim.

If we feel your claim has validity, we will work with you and Our fees are as follows.

Claim amount	Our Fees
Claims under $3500:	$250
$3,500.01 - $5,000	$400
$5000.0 1 — $10,000	$500
$10,000.01 — $20,000	$600
$20,000.01 — $50,000	$700
$50,000.01 - $100,000	$1,000
$100,000.01 — $250,000	$2,000
Over $250,000	custom pricing

Once we have the information that we need we will ask you to forward the following information and documents to us via email or fax.

- A copy of the estimate from your insurance company
- a copy of your insurance policy
- all photographs of the property and damage
- a complete layout of the home with measurements

With this information we can provide you with everything you will need to make sure that you are paid what you are entitled to under your policy. We will provide you with written documentation as well as consult with you via telephone to explain each step that you are to take. We will give you the questions to ask your adjuster, your contractor and even if you are considering hiring a PA or an attorney.

We will advise you as to the verbiage to use when talking to these entities.

You may call us as much as you want or as needed in order to bring your claim to a successful conclusion.

The only thing that we ask you to do is exactly what we ask you to do, no more no less. You do this and we will make your life in dealing with this claim a lot easier.

All payments of fees are made via PayPal

Insurance Claim Worksheet

Part 1

Date of Loss: _____
What caused the loss?_____

Is the home livable?
Do you need a hotel, clothes, food?

Deductible Amount: $_____
Cost of repairs estimate: $_____
Difference: $_____

Is it worth filing a claim? If so, go to part 2

Part 2

Insurance Carrier Phone:_____
Claim number:_____
Adjuster Name:_____
Phone:_____
Email:_____

Contractor name:_____
Phone:_____
Email:_____

For questions or to contact please email us at: wwadjuster@yahoo.com

www.ingramcontent.com/pod-product-compliance
Lightning Source LLC
Chambersburg PA
CBHW031514210526
45464CB00007B/2913